W9-BCR-487

STEP BY STEP PROJECTS

How to Build a BiRdHOUSE

Colleen Hord

Rourke
Educational Media

rourkeeducationalmedia.com

Scan for Related Titles
and Teacher Resources

Teaching Focus:
Consonant Blends- Look in the book to find words that begin with a consonant blend such as *st, tr,* or *gr.*

Before Reading:

Building Academic Vocabulary and Background Knowledge
Before reading a book, it is important to set the stage for your child or student by using pre-reading strategies. This will help them develop their vocabulary, increase their reading comprehension, and make connections across the curriculum.

1. Read the title and look at the cover. *Let's make predictions about what this book will be about.*
2. Take a picture walk by talking about the pictures/photographs in the book. Implant the vocabulary as you take the picture walk. Be sure to talk about the text features such as headings, Table of Contents, glossary, bolded words, captions, charts/diagrams, and Index.
3. Have students read the first page of text with you then have students read the remaining text.
4. Strategy Talk – use to assist students while reading.
   - Get your mouth ready
   - Look at the picture
   - Think…does it make sense
   - Think…does it look right
   - Think…does it sound right
   - Chunk it – by looking for a part you know
5. Read it again.
6. After reading the book complete the activities below.

Content Area Vocabulary

fledgling
habitats
Jenny wren
robin
twigs
twine

After Reading:

Comprehension and Extension Activity
After reading the book, work on the following questions with your child or students in order to check their level of reading comprehension and content mastery.

1. *Why are birdhouses important?* (Summarize)
2. *What types of birds would visit your birdhouse?* (Text to self connection)
3. *Why should you wash and dry the carton before turning it into a birdhouse?* (Asking questions)
4. *Why would other animals want to use the birdhouse?* (Infer)

Extension Activity
Now that you made a birdhouse, how about a bird feeder to go with it! You will need a cardboard roll, peanut butter or honey, bird seed, nail, string, and a butter knife. With the help of an adult, use the butter knife to spread peanut butter or honey all over the outside of the cardboard tube. Next, roll the tube in the bird seed. Try to cover the tube completely. Use the nail to poke a hole in the tube and tie a piece of string through it. Hang your bird feeder by your new birdhouse!

Table of Contents

Birds and Birdhouses

Jenny and Robin may be living in your backyard!

No, they're not people, they are names of birds.

Jenny wren

robin

A **Jenny wren** and a **robin** are just some of the small backyard birds that will build nests in a birdhouse.

Birdhouses are important for birds because many of their **habitats** such as trees, bushes, and tall grasses have been destroyed by construction.

Cutting down trees to build homes or other buildings makes it harder for birds to find places to nest.

People build birdhouses so birds have a safe place to nest. You can help birds by building a birdhouse for your yard.

Birdhouses, just like the houses people live in, come in all colors and sizes.

Gathering Supplies

The first step to building a birdhouse is gathering supplies.

A clean milk carton

Masking tape

Twine

Staples

Acrylic paint

Paintbrush

Scissors

A nail

Building Your Birdhouse

First, wash and dry the carton. Then, staple the top of the carton closed.

Take strips of masking tape and cover the carton. Next, paint the carton.

Once the paint is dry, cut a hole into the middle of one side, large enough for a bird.

Be safe! Never use knives or sharp objects without help from an adult.

Next, take the nail and poke a few holes in the top of the carton to let fresh air in.

Finally, poke a hole in the top of the carton. Pull the **twine** through the hole and tie a knot.

Setting Up Your Birdhouse

Hang your birdhouse on a sturdy tree branch, high enough so animals can't reach it.

Bird watching

Birds will gather **twigs** and grass to build their nests in the birdhouse. You may even see a baby bird, or **fledgling**, poke its head out of the hole!

Keep a watchful eye on your birdhouse. You just might discover Robin and Jenny living in your backyard!

Photo Glossary

fledgling (FLEJ-ling): A baby bird.

habitats (HAB-uh-tats): An animal's natural place to live in nature.

Jenny wren (JEHnee REN): A small, brown songbird with a tail that sticks up.

robin (ROB-in): A songbird with a reddish-orange chest.

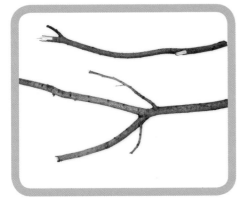

twigs (TWIGS): Small, thin branches of a tree.

twine (TWINE): A very strong string made of two or more strands.

Index

Websites to Visit

www.audubon.org/educate/kids
www.kids.nationalgeographic.com
www.kidsplanet.org

Meet The Author!
www.meetREMauthors.com

About the Author

Colleen Hord is an elementary teacher. Her favorite part of her teaching day is Writer's Workshop. She enjoys kayaking, walking on the beach, and watching the birds that nest on her five acres.

© 2016 Rourke Educational Media

All rights reserved. No part of this book may be reproduced or utilized in any form or by any means, electronic or mechanical including photocopying, recording, or by any information storage and retrieval system without permission in writing from the publisher.

www.rourkeeducationalmedia.com

PHOTO CREDITS: All photography by Lisa Marshall Photography except page 4-5 © CreativeNature R.Zwerver, inset photo © Rob Francis; page 6-7 © Blanscape; page 9 © Budimir Jevtic; page 20 © Cindy underwood; page 22 top © Vishnevskiy Vasily, middle © Tom Reichner, bottom © CreativeNature R.Zwerver; page 23 top © Piotr Krzeslak, page 23 middle © All For You

Edited by: Keli Sipperley
Cover design, interior design and art direction: Nicola Stratford
www.nicolastratford.com

Library of Congress PCN Data

How to Build a Birdhouse/ Colleen Hord
(Step-By-Step Projects)
ISBN 978-1-63430-354-5 (hard cover)
ISBN 978-1-63430-454-2 (soft cover)
ISBN 978-1-63430-552-5 (e-Book)
Library of Congress Control Number: 2014934349

Rourke Educational Media
Printed in the United States of America, North Mankato, Minnesota

Also Available as: